My First Words
A - Z
English to Dutch

Bilingual Learning Made Fun and Easy with Words and Pictures

by Sharon Purtill

Books

Boeken

Mijn eerste woorden
Engels naar Nederlands

My First Words A-Z
English to Dutch

Bilingual Learning Made Fun and
Easy with Words and Pictures

by Sharon Purtill

Published by Dunhill Clare Publishing - Ontario, Canada
Copyright 2021 Dunhill Clare Publishing
dunhillclare@gmail.com

All rights reserved. No part of this publication may be reproduced, stored in a retrieval system or transmitted, in any form or by any means, electronic, mechanical, photocopying, recording or otherwise without the prior permission of the copyright holder except when embodied in a brief review or mention.

Paperback edition   ISBN: 978-1-989733-96-7
Digital edition   ISBN: 978-1-989733-97-4

Library and Archives Canada Cataloguing in Publications

Apple

Appel

Books

Boeken

Cat

Kat

Dog

Hond

Elephant

Olifant

Flower

Bloem

Giraffe

Giraffe

Hat

Hoed

Ice Cream

Ijsje

Jacket

Jas

Keys

Sleutels

Leaf

Blad

Milk

Melk

Nest

Nest

Orange

Sinaasappel

Pail

Emmer

Quilt

Quilt

Rabbit

Konijn

Shoe

Schoen

Table

Tafel

Umbrella

Paraplu

Vacuum Cleaner

Stofzuiger

Watermelon

Watermeloen

Xylophone

Xylofoon

Yellow

Geel

Zebra

Zebra

Bonus Words

English and Dutch

Let's learn common words for items found in and around the home.

oh what FUN

Found in the Kitchen
Wat komen we tegen in de keuken?

plate		bord
fork		vork
spoon		lepel
knife		mes
bowl		kom
cup		glas

Found in the Bathroom
Wat komen we tegen in de badkamer?

toothpaste		tandpasta
toothbrush		tandenborstel
brush		borstel
comb		kam
towel		handdoek

Found in the Bedroom
Wat komen we tegen in de slaapkamer?

bed		bed
blankets		dekens
pillow		kussen
dresser		dressoir
toys		speelgoed

Found in the Living Room
Wat komen we tegen in de woonkamer?

television	televisie
chair	stoel
rug	tapijt
lamp	lamp
sofa	bank

Found Outside
Wat komen we buiten tegen?

tree  boom

car  auto

truck  vrachtauto

bike  fiets

grass  gras

www.ingramcontent.com/pod-product-compliance
Lightning Source LLC
Chambersburg PA
CBHW061202070526
44579CB00009B/109